perfect **pasta**

Easy dishes to cook at home

This edition published in 2010
LOVE FOOD is an imprint of Parragon Books Ltd

Parragon
Queen Street House
4 Queen Street
Bath BA1 1HE, UK

ISBN: 978-1-4075-8105-7

Printed in China

Designed by Talking Design
Cover text and introduction by Lorraine Turner

Notes for the reader
This book uses imperial, metric, and US cup measurements. Follow the same units of
measurement throughout; do not mix imperial and metric. All spoon measurements
are level: teaspoons are assumed to be 5 ml, and tablespoons are assumed to be 15 ml.
Unless otherwise stated, milk is assumed to be whole, eggs and individual vegetables,
such as potatoes, are medium, and pepper is freshly ground black pepper.

The times given are an approximate guide only. Preparation times differ according
to the techniques used by different people and the cooking times may also vary from
those given as a result of the type of oven used. Optional ingredients, variations, or
serving suggestions have not been included in the calculations.

Recipes using raw or very lightly cooked eggs should be avoided by infants, the elderly,
pregnant women, convalescents, and anyone with a chronic condition. Pregnant and
breastfeeding women are advised to avoid eating peanuts and peanut products. People
with nut allergies should be aware that some of the prepared ingredients used in the
recipes in this book may contain nuts. Always check the packaging before use.

Vegetarians should be aware that some of the prepared ingredients used in the recipes
in this book may contain animal products. Always check the packaging before use.

Contents

introduction

It is tempting to think of pasta as a modern food, but its earliest use can been traced to an Etruscan tomb some 30 miles/50 kilometers from Rome. The tomb dates back to around 400BC, and shows the Etruscans making a kind of lasagna. In those days they probably used spelt, a cereal similar to wheat, but hardier and easier to store.

We know that the ancient Romans made lasagna. By the 13th century macaroni was in widespread use in Italy, and by the 17th century pasta had spread to Europe. It is said that President Thomas Jefferson fell in love with macaroni on a visit to Naples in the 18th century and introduced it to the people of the United States. From there it flourished even more and became a firm favorite all over the world.

Today, variations of this popular food can be found all around the globe. For example, the Chinese have perfected the use of egg noodles in stir-fries, and the Spanish use wonderfully fine, vermicelli-like noodles called "*fideos.*" These are particularly delicious added to clear soups and make them more substantial and satisfying.

Pasta is unparalleled for its versatility. It is very easy to make at home, although commercially available pasta is of such high quality that it is no longer necessary to make it yourself. It comes in a very wide range of shapes and sizes, from long noodles and rectangular sheets, to bows, spirals, and shells.

Preparing and cooking pasta

It is very easy and quick to prepare and cook pasta, so this food is ideal for the novice and more experienced cook alike. It is also very handy if you are short of time. Fresh unfilled pasta needs only 3 minutes to cook, or 10 minutes if it is filled. For example, you would need to boil fresh fettuccine (long noodles) in water for only 3 minutes, or fresh ravioli (filled pasta "cushions") for 10 minutes.

If you are using dried pasta, you will need to cook it for 8–10 minutes if it is unfilled, and 15–20 minutes if it is filled.

Enticing accompaniments

Pasta is delicious served on its own, simply seasoned with salt and freshly ground black pepper and drizzled with olive oil. However, it also makes the perfect partner for a wide range of delicious and exciting sauces. Top a platter of freshly cooked spaghetti with a rich tomato and beef sauce, for example, and you have the classic Spaghetti Bolognese, or why not try omitting the beef from the tomato sauce and creating a Spaghetti Napoletana for vegetarians?

You can top your pasta with cream-based sauces, or sauces using meat, fish, or vegetables, so the combinations are truly endless. Simply scatter over some freshly grated Parmesan cheese, perhaps add an accompaniment of some garlic bread, warmed

in the oven, and you have an irresistible meal to tempt the most discerning palate.

Essential equipment

You don't need any special equipment to prepare and cook pasta, just a large saucepan for boiling the pasta in water, and one or two heatproof dishes for baked pasta recipes, such as lasagna. A pasta ladle has "teeth" around the edge, and is useful for lifting drained pasta noodles onto plates, but is not essential. Likewise, a pasta machine is not vital because store-bought pasta is so good these days, but if you prefer to make your own, you will find it very helpful for rolling out your freshly made pasta and cutting it into ribbons, noodles, and a variety of decorative shapes.

The recipes in this book use a wide variety of dried pasta. However, for the more adventurous cook, follow the recipe below to make your own beautifully fresh version:

Basic Pasta Dough

Serves 3–4
1¾ cups white bread flour, plus extra for dusting
pinch of salt
2 eggs, lightly beaten
1 tbsp olive oil

Sift together the flour and the salt onto a counter and make a well in the center with your fingers. Pour the eggs and oil into the well, then, using the fingers of one hand, gradually incorporate the flour into the liquid.

Knead the dough on a lightly floured counter until it is completely smooth. Wrap in plastic wrap and let rest for 30 minutes before rolling out or feeding through a pasta machine. Resting makes the dough more elastic.

soups & salads

Tortellini
in Broth

SERVES 6

3 tbsp olive oil

1 red onion, finely chopped

2 garlic cloves, finely chopped

12 oz/350 g ground beef

1 tsp finely chopped fresh thyme

1 fresh rosemary sprig, finely
  chopped

1 bay leaf

7½ cups beef stock

2 quantities Basic Pasta Dough
  (see page 5)

all-purpose flour, for dusting

1 egg, lightly beaten

salt and pepper

Heat the oil in a pan. Add the onion and garlic and cook over low heat, stirring occasionally, for 5 minutes, until softened but not browned. Add the beef, increase the heat to medium, and cook, stirring with a wooden spoon to break up the meat, for 8–10 minutes, until evenly browned. Stir in the herbs, season to taste with salt and pepper, add ½ cup of the stock, and bring to a boil. Cover and simmer for 25 minutes, then remove the lid and cook until all the liquid has evaporated. Remove the pan from the heat and discard the bay leaf.

Roll out the pasta dough on a lightly floured surface to ¹⁄16–⅛ inch/ 2–3 mm thick. Using a ¾-inch/2-cm plain cookie cutter, stamp out circles. Place about ¼ teaspoon of the cooled meat mixture in the center of each circle. Brush the edges of each circle with a little beaten egg, then fold them in half to make half moons and press the edges to seal. Wrap a half moon around the tip of your index finger until the corners meet and press together to seal. Repeat with the remaining pasta half moons. Place the filled tortellini on a floured dish towel and let dry for 30 minutes.

Bring the remaining stock to a boil in a large pan. Add the tortellini, bring back to a boil, and cook for 3–4 minutes, until tender but still firm to the bite. Ladle the tortellini and broth into warmed soup bowls and serve immediately.

Pasta Salad
with Walnuts & Gorgonzola

SERVES 4

8 oz/225 g dried farfalle (pasta bows)

2 tbsp walnut oil

4 tbsp safflower oil

2 tbsp balsamic vinegar

10 oz/280 g mixed salad greens

8 oz/225 g Gorgonzola cheese, diced

½ cup walnut halves, toasted

salt and pepper

Bring a large, heavy-bottom pan of lightly salted water to a boil. Add the pasta, bring back to a boil, and cook for 8–10 minutes, or until tender but still firm to the bite. Drain and refresh in a bowl of cold water. Drain again.

Mix the walnut oil, safflower oil, and vinegar together in a measuring cup, whisking well, and season to taste with salt and pepper.

Arrange the salad greens in a large serving bowl. Top with the pasta, Gorgonzola cheese, and walnuts. Pour the dressing over the salad, toss lightly, and serve.

Fish Soup
with Macaroni

SERVES 6

2 tbsp olive oil

2 onions, sliced

1 garlic clove, finely chopped

4 cups fish stock or water

14 oz/400 g canned chopped
 tomatoes

¼ tsp herbes de Provence

¼ tsp saffron threads

4 oz/115 g dried macaroni

18 mussels, scrubbed and debearded

1 lb/450 g monkfish fillet, cut into
 chunks

8 oz/225 g raw jumbo shrimp, shelled
 and deveined, tails left on

salt and pepper

Heat the oil in a large, heavy-bottom pan. Add the onions and garlic and cook over low heat, stirring occasionally, for 5 minutes, or until the onions have softened.

Add the stock with the tomatoes and their can juices, herbes de Provence, saffron, and pasta, and season to taste with salt and pepper. Bring to a boil, then cover and simmer for 15 minutes.

Discard any mussels with broken shells and any that refuse to close when tapped. Add the mussels, monkfish, and shrimp to the pan. Re-cover and simmer for an additional 5–10 minutes, until the mussels have opened, the shrimp have changed color, and the fish is opaque and flakes easily. Discard any mussels that remain closed. Ladle the soup into warmed bowls and serve.

Pasta & Potato Soup
with Pesto

SERVES 4

2 tbsp olive oil

3 strips smoked, fatty bacon,
   chopped

2 tbsp butter

1 lb/450 g starchy potatoes,
   finely chopped

1 lb/450 g onions, finely chopped

2½ cups chicken stock

2½ cups milk

3½ oz/100 g dried conchigliette
   (small pasta shells)

⅔ cup heavy cream

2 tbsp chopped fresh parsley

2 tbsp pesto

salt and pepper

fresh Parmesan cheese shavings,
   to serve

Heat the oil in a large pan and cook the bacon over medium heat for 4 minutes. Add the butter, potatoes, and onions, and cook for 12 minutes, stirring constantly.

Add the stock and milk to the pan, bring to a boil, and simmer for 5 minutes. Add the pasta and simmer for an additional 3–5 minutes.

Stir in the cream and simmer for 5 minutes. Add the parsley, pesto, and salt and pepper to taste. Transfer the soup to individual serving bowls and serve with Parmesan cheese shavings.

Pasta Salad
with Bell Peppers

SERVES 4

1 red bell pepper

1 orange bell pepper

10 oz/280 g dried conchiglie
(pasta shells)

5 tbsp extra virgin olive oil

2 tbsp lemon juice

2 tbsp pesto

1 garlic clove, very finely chopped

3 tbsp shredded fresh basil leaves

salt and pepper

Put the whole bell peppers on a baking sheet and place under a preheated broiler, turning frequently, for 15 minutes, until charred all over. Remove with tongs and place in a bowl. Cover with crumpled paper towels and set aside.

Meanwhile, bring a large pan of lightly salted water to a boil. Add the pasta, bring back to a boil, and cook for 8–10 minutes, until tender but still firm to the bite.

Combine the oil, lemon juice, pesto, and garlic in a bowl, whisking well to mix. Drain the pasta, add it to the pesto mixture while still hot, and toss well. Set aside.

When the bell peppers are cool enough to handle, peel off the skins, then cut open and remove the seeds. Chop the flesh coarsely and add to the pasta mixture with the basil. Season to taste with salt and pepper and toss well. Serve at room temperature.

Rare Beef
with Pasta Salad

SERVES 4

1 lb/450 g sirloin or porterhouse
   steak in 1 piece
1 lb/450 g dried fusilli (pasta spirals)
4 tbsp olive oil
2 tbsp lime juice
2 tbsp Thai fish sauce
2 tsp honey
4 scallions, sliced
1 cucumber, peeled and cut into
   1-inch/2.5-cm chunks
3 tomatoes, cut into wedges
3 tsp finely chopped fresh mint
salt and pepper

Season the steak with salt and pepper to taste. Broil or pan-fry the steak for about 4 minutes on each side. Let stand for 5 minutes, then slice thinly across the grain.

Meanwhile, bring a large pan of lightly salted water to a boil over medium heat. Add the pasta, bring back to a boil, and cook for 8–10 minutes, or until tender but still firm to the bite. Drain the pasta thoroughly, then refresh in cold water and drain again. Return the pasta to the pan and toss in the oil.

Mix the lime juice, fish sauce, and honey together in a small pan and cook over medium heat for about 2 minutes.

Add the scallions, cucumber, tomatoes, and mint to the pan, then add the steak and mix well. Season to taste with salt.

Transfer the pasta to a large, warmed serving dish and top with the steak mixture. Serve just warm or let cool completely.

Niçoise
Pasta Salad

SERVES 4

12 oz/350 g dried conchiglie
 (pasta shells)
4 oz/115 g green beans
1¾ oz/50 g canned anchovy fillets,
 drained
2 tbsp milk
2 small heads of crisp lettuce
3 large tomatoes
4 hard-cooked eggs
8 oz/225 g canned tuna, drained
1 cup pitted ripe black olives
salt

Vinaigrette Dressing

¼ cup extra virgin olive oil
2 tbsp white wine vinegar
1 tsp whole grain mustard
salt and pepper

Bring a large pan of lightly salted water to a boil over medium heat. Add the pasta, bring back to a boil, and cook for 8–10 minutes, or until tender but still firm to the bite. Drain the pasta thoroughly and refresh in cold water.

Bring a small pan of lightly salted water to a boil over medium heat. Add the beans and cook for 10–12 minutes, or until done. Drain thoroughly and refresh in cold water, then drain again and set aside.

Put the anchovies into a shallow bowl, then pour over the milk and set aside for 10 minutes. Meanwhile, tear the lettuce into large pieces. Blanch the tomatoes in boiling water for 1–2 minutes, then drain. Skin and coarsely chop the flesh. Shell the eggs and cut into quarters. Flake the tuna into large chunks.

Drain the anchovies and the pasta. Put all the salad ingredients into a large bowl and gently mix together.

To make the vinaigrette dressing, beat the oil, vinegar, and mustard together, season to taste with salt and pepper, and keep in the refrigerator until ready to serve. Just before serving, pour the vinaigrette dressing over the salad and toss well.

meat & poultry

Spaghetti
Bolognese

SERVES 4

1 tbsp olive oil

1 onion, finely chopped

2 garlic cloves, chopped

1 carrot, chopped

1 celery stalk, chopped

1¾ oz/50 g pancetta or bacon, diced

12 oz/350 g lean ground beef

14 oz/400 g canned chopped
   tomatoes

2 tsp dried oregano

½ cup red wine

2 tbsp tomato paste

12 oz/350 g dried spaghetti

salt and pepper

chopped fresh flat-leaf parsley,
   to garnish

Heat the oil in a large skillet. Add the onion and cook for 3 minutes. Add the garlic, carrot, celery, and pancetta and sauté for 3–4 minutes, or until just beginning to brown.

Add the beef and cook over high heat for 3 minutes, or until all of the meat is browned. Stir in the tomatoes, oregano, and red wine and bring to a boil. Reduce the heat and simmer for about 45 minutes. Stir in the tomato paste and season to taste with salt and pepper.

Meanwhile, bring a large, heavy-bottom pan of lightly salted water to a boil. Add the pasta, bring back to a boil, and cook for 8–10 minutes, or until tender but still firm to the bite. Drain thoroughly.

Transfer the spaghetti to a serving plate and pour over the bolognese sauce. Toss to mix well, garnish with parsley, and serve hot.

Spaghetti
alla Carbonara

SERVES 4

1 lb/450 g dried spaghetti

1 tbsp olive oil

8 oz/225 g rindless pancetta or lean
   bacon, chopped

4 eggs

5 tbsp light cream

2 tbsp freshly grated Parmesan
   cheese

salt and pepper

Bring a large, heavy-bottom pan of lightly salted water to a boil. Add the pasta, bring back to a boil, and cook for 8–10 minutes, or until tender but still firm to the bite.

Meanwhile, heat the oil in a heavy-bottom skillet. Add the pancetta and cook over medium heat, stirring frequently, for 8–10 minutes.

Beat the eggs with the cream in a small bowl and season to taste with salt and pepper. Drain the pasta and return it to the pan. Turn in the contents of the skillet, then add the egg mixture and half the Parmesan cheese. Stir well, then transfer to a warmed serving dish. Serve immediately, sprinkled with the remaining cheese.

Pepperoni
Pasta

SERVES 4

3 tbsp olive oil

1 onion, chopped

1 red bell pepper, seeded and diced

1 orange bell pepper, seeded and
diced

1 lb 12 oz/800 g canned chopped
tomatoes

1 tbsp sun-dried tomato paste

1 tsp paprika

8 oz/225 g pepperoni sausage, sliced

2 tbsp chopped fresh flat-leaf parsley,
plus extra to garnish

1 lb/450 g dried penne (pasta quills)

salt and pepper

Heat 2 tablespoons of the oil in a large, heavy-bottom skillet. Add the onion and cook over low heat, stirring occasionally, for 5 minutes, or until softened. Add the red and orange bell peppers, tomatoes and their can juices, sun-dried tomato paste, and paprika and bring to a boil.

Add the pepperoni and parsley and season to taste with salt and pepper. Stir well, bring to a boil, then reduce the heat and simmer for 10–15 minutes.

Meanwhile, bring a large, heavy-bottom pan of lightly salted water to a boil. Add the pasta, bring back to a boil, and cook for 8–10 minutes, or until tender but still firm to the bite. Drain well and transfer to a warmed serving dish. Add the remaining oil and toss. Add the sauce and toss again. Garnish with parsley and serve immediately.

Farfalle
with Gorgonzola & Ham

SERVES 4

1 cup sour cream

8 oz/225 g cremini mushrooms,
  quartered

14 oz/400 g dried farfalle
  (pasta bows)

3 oz/85 g Gorgonzola cheese,
  crumbled

1 tbsp chopped fresh flat-leaf parsley,
  plus extra sprigs to garnish

1 cup diced cooked ham

salt and pepper

Pour the sour cream into a pan, add the mushrooms, and season to taste with salt and pepper. Bring to just below a boil, then reduce the heat and simmer very gently, stirring occasionally, for 8–10 minutes, until the cream has thickened.

Meanwhile, bring a large pan of lightly salted water to a boil. Add the pasta, bring back to a boil, and cook for 8–10 minutes, until tender but still firm to the bite.

Remove the pan of mushrooms from the heat and stir in the cheese until it has melted. Return the pan to low heat and stir in the chopped parsley and ham.

Drain the pasta and add it to the sauce. Toss lightly, then divide among individual warmed plates. Garnish with parsley sprigs and serve.

Tagliatelle
with Spring Lamb

SERVES 4

1 lb 10 oz/750 g boneless lean lamb in a single piece

6 garlic cloves, thinly sliced

6–8 fresh rosemary sprigs

½ cup olive oil

14 oz/400 g dried tagliatelle

4 tbsp butter

6 oz/175 g button mushrooms

salt and pepper

fresh Parmesan cheese shavings, to serve

Using a sharp knife, cut small pockets all over the lamb, then insert a garlic slice and a few rosemary leaves in each one. Heat 2 tablespoons of the oil in a large, heavy-bottom skillet. Add the lamb and cook over medium heat, turning occasionally, for 25–30 minutes, until tender and cooked to your liking. Remove the lamb from the heat, cover with foil, and let stand.

Meanwhile, chop the remaining rosemary and place in a mortar. Add the remaining oil and pound with a pestle. Season to taste with salt and pepper and set aside.

Bring a large pan of lightly salted water to a boil. Add the pasta, bring back to a boil, and cook for 8–10 minutes, until tender but still firm to the bite.

Melt the butter in a separate pan. Add the mushrooms and cook over low–medium heat, stirring occasionally, for 5–8 minutes.

Drain the pasta, return it to the pan, and toss with half the rosemary oil. Uncover the lamb and cut it into slices. Divide the tagliatelle among individual warmed plates and top with the lamb and mushrooms. Drizzle with the remaining rosemary oil, sprinkle with the Parmesan cheese shavings, and serve immediately.

Pappardelle
with Chicken & Porcini

SERVES 4

½ cup dried porcini mushrooms

¾ cup hot water

1 lb 12 oz/800 g canned chopped
   tomatoes

1 fresh red chile, seeded and finely
   chopped

3 tbsp olive oil

12 oz/350 g skinless, boneless chicken
   breasts, cut into thin strips

2 garlic cloves, finely chopped

12 oz/350 g dried pappardelle

salt and pepper

2 tbsp chopped fresh flat-leaf parsley,
   to garnish

Place the porcini in a small bowl, add the hot water, and let soak for 20 minutes. Meanwhile, place the tomatoes and their can juices in a heavy-bottom pan and break them up with a wooden spoon, then stir in the chile. Bring to a boil, reduce the heat, and simmer, stirring occasionally, for 30 minutes, or until reduced.

Remove the mushrooms from their soaking liquid with a slotted spoon, reserving the liquid. Strain the liquid through a coffee filter paper or cheesecloth-lined strainer into the tomatoes and simmer for an additional 15 minutes.

Heat 2 tablespoons of the oil in a heavy-bottom skillet. Add the chicken and cook, stirring frequently, until golden brown all over and tender. Stir in the mushrooms and garlic and cook for 5 minutes.

Meanwhile, bring a large, heavy-bottom pan of lightly salted water to a boil. Add the pasta, bring back to a boil, and cook for 8–10 minutes, or until tender but still firm to the bite. Drain well, transfer to a warmed serving dish, drizzle with the remaining oil, and toss lightly.

Stir the chicken mixture into the tomato sauce, season to taste with salt and pepper, and spoon onto the pasta. Toss lightly, garnish with parsley, and serve immediately.

fish & seafood

Spaghetti
alla Puttanesca

SERVES 4

3 tbsp olive oil

2 garlic cloves, finely chopped

10 canned anchovy fillets, drained
   and chopped

1 cup black olives, pitted and
   chopped

1 tbsp capers, drained and rinsed

1 lb/450 g plum tomatoes, peeled,
   seeded, and chopped

cayenne pepper, to taste

14 oz/400 g dried spaghetti

salt

2 tbsp chopped fresh parsley,
   to garnish (optional)

Heat the oil in a heavy-bottom skillet. Add the garlic and cook over low heat, stirring frequently, for 2 minutes. Add the anchovies and mash them to a pulp with a fork. Add the olives, capers, and tomatoes, and season to taste with cayenne pepper. Cover and simmer for 25 minutes.

Meanwhile, bring a large, heavy-bottom pan of lightly salted water to a boil. Add the pasta, bring back to a boil, and cook for 8–10 minutes, or until tender but still firm to the bite. Drain well and transfer to a warmed serving dish.

Spoon the anchovy sauce into the dish and toss the pasta, using 2 large forks. Garnish with parsley, if using, and serve immediately.

Spaghetti
with Tuna & Parsley

SERVES 6

1 lb 2 oz/500 g dried spaghetti

2 tbsp butter

7 oz/200 g canned tuna, drained

2 oz/55 g canned anchovies, drained

1 cup olive oil

1 cup coarsely chopped fresh flat-leaf
  parsley

2/3 cup sour cream or yogurt

salt and pepper

Bring a large, heavy-bottom pan of lightly salted water to a boil. Add the spaghetti, bring back to a boil, and cook for 8–10 minutes, or until tender but still firm to the bite. Drain the spaghetti and return to the pan. Add the butter, toss thoroughly to coat, and keep warm until needed.

Flake the tuna into smaller pieces using 2 forks. Place the tuna in a food processor or blender with the anchovies, oil, and parsley and process until the sauce is smooth. Pour in the sour cream and process for a few seconds to blend. Taste the sauce and adjust the seasoning, adding salt and pepper, if necessary.

Shake the pan of spaghetti over medium heat for a few minutes, or until it is thoroughly warmed through.

Pour the sauce over the spaghetti and toss quickly, using 2 forks. Serve immediately.

Springtime
Pasta

SERVES 4

2 tbsp lemon juice

4 baby globe artichokes

7 tbsp olive oil

2 shallots, finely chopped

2 garlic cloves, finely chopped

2 tbsp chopped fresh flat-leaf parsley

2 tbsp chopped fresh mint

12 oz/350 g dried rigatoni
  (pasta tubes)

12 large raw shrimp

2 tbsp butter

salt and pepper

Fill a bowl with cold water and add the lemon juice. Prepare the artichokes one at a time. Cut off the stems and trim away any tough outer leaves. Cut across the tops of the leaves. Slice in half lengthwise and remove the central fibrous chokes, then cut lengthwise into ¼ inch/5 mm thick slices. Immediately place the slices in the bowl of acidulated water to prevent discoloration.

Heat 5 tablespoons of the oil in a heavy-bottom skillet. Drain the artichoke slices and pat dry with paper towels. Add them to the skillet with the shallots, garlic, parsley, and mint, and cook over low heat, stirring frequently, for 10–12 minutes, until tender.

Meanwhile, bring a large pan of lightly salted water to a boil. Add the pasta, bring back to a boil, and cook for 8–10 minutes, until tender but still firm to the bite.

Shell the shrimp, then remove and discard the dark vein. Melt the butter in a small skillet and add the shrimp. Cook, stirring occasionally, for 2–3 minutes, until they have changed color. Season to taste with salt and pepper.

Drain the pasta and transfer it to a bowl. Add the remaining oil and toss well. Add the artichoke mixture and the shrimp and toss again. Serve immediately.

Linguine
with Shrimp & Scallops

SERVES 6

1 lb/450 g raw jumbo shrimp

2 tbsp butter

2 shallots, finely chopped

1 cup dry white vermouth

1½ cups water

1 lb/450 g dried linguine

2 tbsp olive oil

1 lb/450 g prepared scallops, thawed
   if frozen

2 tbsp snipped fresh chives

salt and pepper

Shell the shrimp, reserving the shells, and remove and discard the dark vein. Melt the butter in a heavy-bottom skillet. Add the shallots and cook over low heat, stirring occasionally, for 5 minutes, or until softened. Add the shrimp shells and cook, stirring constantly, for 1 minute. Pour in the vermouth and cook, stirring, for 1 minute. Add the water, bring to a boil, then reduce the heat and simmer for 10 minutes, or until the liquid has reduced by half. Remove the skillet from the heat.

Bring a large, heavy-bottom pan of lightly salted water to a boil. Add the pasta, bring back to a boil, and cook for 8–10 minutes, or until tender but still firm to the bite.

Meanwhile, heat the oil in a separate heavy-bottom skillet. Add the scallops and shrimp and cook, stirring frequently, for 2 minutes, or until the scallops are opaque and the shrimp have changed color. Strain the shrimp-shell stock into the skillet. Drain the pasta and add to the skillet with the chives and season to taste with salt and pepper. Toss well over low heat for 1 minute, then serve.

Fusilli with
Monkfish & Broccoli

SERVES 4

4 oz/115 g broccoli, separated into
   florets
3 tbsp olive oil
12 oz/350 g monkfish fillet, skinned
   and cut into bite-size pieces
2 garlic cloves, crushed
½ cup dry white wine
1 cup heavy cream
14 oz/400 g dried fusilli
   (pasta spirals)
3 oz/85 g Gorgonzola cheese, diced
salt and pepper

Separate the broccoli florets into tiny sprigs.
Bring a pan of lightly salted water to a boil, add
the broccoli, and cook for 2 minutes. Drain and
refresh under cold running water.

Heat the oil in a large, heavy-bottom skillet. Add
the monkfish and garlic and season to taste with salt and pepper.
Cook, stirring frequently, for 5 minutes, or until the fish is opaque. Pour
in the wine and cream and cook, stirring occasionally, for 5 minutes,
or until the fish is cooked through and the sauce has thickened. Stir in
the broccoli.

Meanwhile, bring a large, heavy-bottom pan of lightly salted water to
a boil. Add the pasta, bring back to a boil, and cook for 8–10 minutes, or
until tender but still firm to the bite. Drain and turn the pasta into the
pan with the fish, add the cheese, and toss lightly. Serve immediately.

Penne with
Squid & Tomatoes

SERVES 4

8 oz/225 g dried penne (pasta quills)

12 oz/350 g prepared squid

6 tbsp olive oil

2 onions, sliced

1 cup fish or chicken stock

2/3 cup full-bodied red wine

14 oz/400 g canned chopped
   tomatoes

2 tbsp tomato paste

1 tbsp chopped fresh marjoram

1 bay leaf

salt and pepper

2 tbsp chopped fresh parsley,
   to garnish

Bring a large, heavy-bottom pan of lightly salted water to a boil. Add the pasta, bring back to a boil, and cook for 3 minutes, then drain and set aside until ready to use. With a sharp knife, cut the squid into strips.

Heat the oil in a large pan. Add the onions and cook over low heat, stirring occasionally, for 5 minutes, or until softened. Add the squid and stock, bring to a boil, and simmer for 3 minutes. Stir in the wine, tomatoes and their can juices, tomato paste, marjoram, and bay leaf. Season to taste with salt and pepper. Bring to a boil and cook for 5 minutes, or until slightly reduced.

Add the pasta, return to a boil, and simmer for 5–7 minutes, or until tender but still firm to the bite. Remove and discard the bay leaf. Transfer to a warmed serving dish, garnish with parsley, and serve immediately.

vegetarian

Fettuccine
Alfredo

SERVES 4

2 tbsp butter

1 cup heavy cream

1 lb/450 g dried fettuccine

1 cup freshly grated Parmesan
   cheese, plus extra to serve

pinch of freshly grated nutmeg

salt and pepper

1 fresh flat-leaf parsley sprig,
   to garnish

Put the butter and ⅔ cup of the cream in a large pan and bring the mixture to a boil over medium heat. Reduce the heat, then simmer gently for about 1–2 minutes, or until the cream has thickened slightly.

Meanwhile, bring a large pan of lightly salted water to a boil over medium heat. Add the pasta, bring back to a boil, and cook for 8–10 minutes, or until tender but still firm to the bite. Drain the pasta thoroughly and return to the pan, then pour over the cream sauce.

Toss the pasta in the sauce over low heat until thoroughly coated. Add the remaining cream, the Parmesan cheese, and nutmeg to the pasta mixture and season to taste with salt and pepper. Toss the pasta thoroughly in the mixture while gently heating through.

Transfer the pasta mixture to a large, warmed serving plate and garnish with the fresh parsley sprig. Serve immediately with extra grated Parmesan cheese.

Spaghettini
with Tomatoes & Black Olives

SERVES 4

1 tbsp olive oil

1 garlic clove, finely chopped

2 tsp capers, drained, rinsed, and chopped

12 black olives, pitted and chopped

½ dried red chile, crushed

2 lb 12 oz/1.25 kg canned chopped tomatoes

1 tbsp chopped fresh parsley, plus extra to garnish

12 oz/350 g dried spaghettini

2 tbsp freshly grated Parmesan cheese

salt

Heat the oil in a large, heavy-bottom skillet. Add the garlic and cook over low heat for 30 seconds, then add the capers, olives, chile, and tomatoes, and season to taste with salt. Partially cover the skillet and simmer gently for 20 minutes.

Stir in the parsley, partially cover the skillet again, and simmer for an additional 10 minutes.

Meanwhile, bring a large, heavy-bottom pan of lightly salted water to a boil. Add the pasta, bring back to a boil, and cook for 8–10 minutes, or until tender but still firm to the bite. Drain and transfer to a warmed serving dish. Add the sauce and toss well. Sprinkle over the Parmesan and garnish with extra chopped parsley. Serve immediately.

Olive, Bell Pepper &
Tomato Pasta

SERVES 4

8 oz/225 g dried penne (pasta quills)

2 tbsp olive oil

2 tbsp butter

2 garlic cloves, crushed

1 green bell pepper, seeded and
thinly sliced

1 yellow bell pepper, seeded and
thinly sliced

16 cherry tomatoes, halved

1 tbsp chopped fresh oregano,
plus extra sprigs to garnish

½ cup dry white wine

2 tbsp quartered, pitted black olives

2¾ oz/75 g arugula

salt and pepper

Bring a large, heavy-bottom pan of lightly salted water to a boil. Add the pasta, bring back to a boil, and cook for 8–10 minutes, or until tender but still firm to the bite. Drain the pasta thoroughly.

Heat the oil and butter in a skillet until the butter melts. Cook the garlic for 30 seconds. Add the peppers and cook, stirring constantly, for 3–4 minutes.

Stir in the cherry tomatoes, oregano, wine, and olives, and cook for 3–4 minutes. Season well with salt and pepper and stir in the arugula until just wilted. Transfer the pasta to a serving dish, spoon over the sauce, and garnish with oregano sprigs. Serve.

Rigatoni
with Bell Peppers & Goat Cheese

SERVES 4

2 tbsp olive oil

1 tbsp butter

1 small onion, finely chopped

4 bell peppers, yellow and red,
  seeded and cut into ¾-inch/
  2-cm squares

3 garlic cloves, thinly sliced

1 lb/450 g dried rigatoni
  (pasta tubes)

4½ oz/125 g goat cheese, crumbled

15 fresh basil leaves, shredded

10 black olives, pitted and sliced

salt and pepper

Heat the oil and butter in a large skillet over medium heat. Add the onion and cook until soft. Increase the heat to medium–high and add the bell peppers and garlic. Cook for 12–15 minutes, stirring, until the peppers are tender but not mushy. Season to taste with salt and pepper. Remove from the heat.

Bring a large pan of lightly salted water to a boil. Add the pasta, bring back to a boil, and cook for 8–10 minutes, or until tender but still firm to the bite. Drain and transfer to a warmed serving dish. Add the goat cheese and toss to mix.

Briefly reheat the sauce. Add the basil and olives. Pour over the pasta and toss well to mix. Serve immediately.

Linguine
with Wild Mushrooms

SERVES 4

4 tbsp butter

1 onion, chopped

1 garlic clove, finely chopped

12 oz/350 g wild mushrooms, sliced

12 oz/350 g dried linguine

1¼ cups sour cream

2 tbsp shredded fresh basil leaves, plus extra to garnish

4 tbsp freshly grated Parmesan cheese, plus extra to serve

salt and pepper

Melt the butter in a large, heavy-bottom skillet. Add the onion and garlic and cook over low heat for 5 minutes, or until softened. Add the mushrooms and cook, stirring occasionally, for an additional 10 minutes.

Meanwhile, bring a large, heavy-bottom pan of lightly salted water to a boil. Add the pasta, bring back to a boil, and cook for 8–10 minutes, or until tender but still firm to the bite.

Stir the sour cream, basil, and Parmesan cheese into the mushroom mixture and season to taste with salt and pepper. Cover and heat through gently for 1–2 minutes. Drain the pasta and transfer to a warmed serving dish. Add the mushroom mixture and toss lightly. Garnish with extra basil and serve immediately with extra Parmesan cheese.

Linguine
with Roasted Garlic & Bell Peppers

SERVES 4

6 large garlic cloves, unpeeled

14 oz/400 g bottled roasted red bell
  peppers, drained and sliced

7 oz/200 g canned chopped
  tomatoes

3 tbsp olive oil

¼ tsp dried chile flakes

1 tsp chopped fresh thyme or
  oregano

12 oz/350 g dried linguine

salt and pepper

Preheat the oven to 400°F/200°C. Place the unpeeled garlic cloves in a shallow, ovenproof dish. Roast in the preheated oven for 7–10 minutes, or until the garlic cloves feel soft.

Put the bell peppers, tomatoes, and oil in a food processor or blender, then puree. Squeeze the garlic flesh into the puree. Add the chile flakes and thyme. Season to taste with salt and pepper. Blend again, then scrape into a pan and set aside.

Bring a large saucepan of lightly salted water to a boil. Add the pasta, bring back to a boil, and cook for 8–10 minutes, or until tender but still firm to the bite. Drain and transfer to a warmed serving dish.

Reheat the sauce and pour over the pasta. Toss well to mix and serve immediately.